C000215850

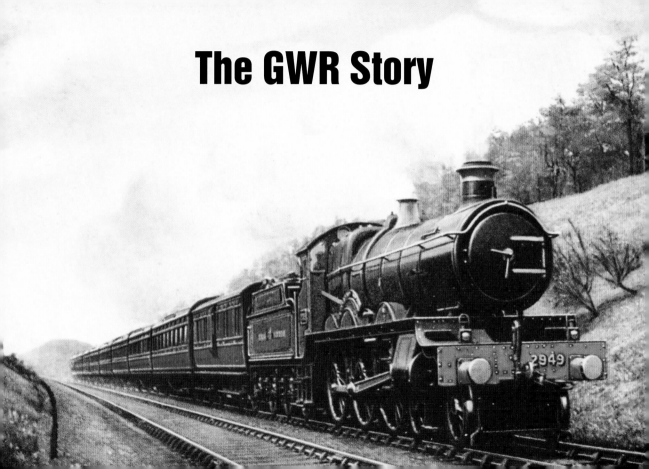

The GWR Story

AEC 10-TON DIESEL RAILCAR of 1938.

The GWR Story

Rosa Matheson

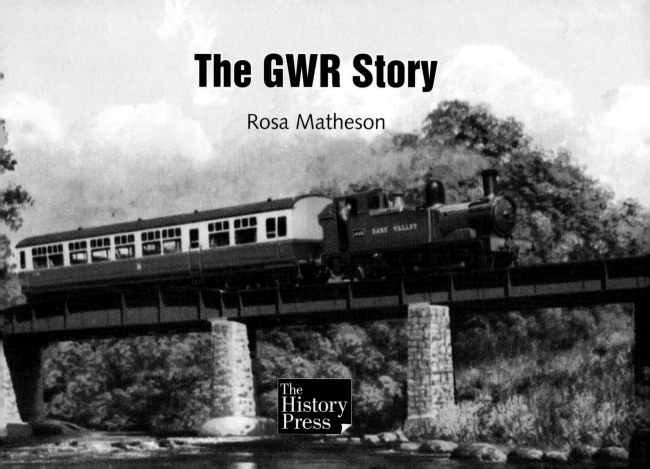

The
History
Press

Published in the United Kingdom in 2010 by
The History Press
The Mill · Brimscombe Port · Stroud · Gloucestershire · GL5 2QG

Copyright © Rosa Matheson, 2010

All rights reserved. No part of this publication may be
reproduced, stored in a retrieval system, or transmitted, in any
form, or by any means, electronic, mechanical, photocopying,
recording or otherwise, without the prior permission of the
publisher and copyright holder.

Rosa Matheson has asserted her moral right to be identified as
the author of this work.

British Library Cataloguing in Publication Data
A catalogue record for this book is available from the British
Library.

Hardback ISBN 978-0-7524-5624-9

Typesetting and origination by The History Press
Printed in Italy by L.E.G.O. S.p.A.

Front cover
*The Birmingham Two-Hour and North Express at
Hatton Summit. GWR's famous 'King' class – four-
cylinder 4-6-0 engine No.6001* King Edward VII.
(David Hyde Collection)

Page 1
'Saint' class two-cylinder 4-6-0 No.2949 Stanford
Court, *the Up-Birmingham Express, c.1912, with
Toplight coaches in Lake Livery. Note the red
roof boards with gold lettering. (Jack Hayward
Collection)*

Miscellaneous Trains
Page 2
*Streamlined Diesel Railcars were introduced in 1933.
Variations followed and in 1936 No.17 appeared
as a parcels car operating out of Paddington. (Great
Western Trust Collection)*

Page 3
*The 'Auto-train' was a development for use on
branch line-services brought in to compete with
the introduction of buses in an attempt to retain
rail-passengers. These trains could be driven from
either end, carriage or locomotive. (Jack Hayward
Collection)*

A G.W.R. STANDARD MONOGRAM.

A STANDARD monogram, displaying the initials " G.W.R." in a circle, has been adopted by the Great Western Railway Company. This will take the place of the words " Great Western Railway," the Company's crest, and various other combinations and abbreviations.

This simple, stylistic and now immediately recognisable monogram was introduced in 1934.

CONTENTS

C. W. R. LOCOMOTIVES
REPRODUCED TO THE SAME SCALE

"NORTH STAR" ——— —— ——— — AS CONSTRUCTED BY R. STEPHENSON & CO. IN 1837.
"LORD OF THE ISLES" —— —— —— — BUILT BY C. W. R. CO. AT SWINDON IN 1851.
"KING GEORGE V" —— —— —— — DO. DO. DO. DO. DO. 1927.

| ENGINE | CYLINDERS | | DRIVING WHEELS | BOILER PRESSURE | TRACTIVE EFFORT AT 85% BOILER PRESSURE |
	Nº	DIMENSIONS			
"NORTH STAR"	2	16" x 16"	7'—0"	50 LBS.	2070 LBS.
"LORD OF THE ISLES"	2	18" x 24"	8'—0"	140 "	9640 "
"KING GEORGE V"	4	16¼" x 28"	6'—6"	250 "	40300 "

6

Whilst my collaborators on this work have been few, their efforts and contributions have been immense. Thanks to Adrian Vaughan, Revd Canon Brian Arman and David Hyde for generously giving expert scrutiny, technical advice and information, and to David, Phil Kelley, Eddie Lyons and Jack Hayward for their research. A huge vote of thanks for pictorial content to David Hyde for GWR photographs and publicity, the Great Western Trust, Brian Arman, Bob Townsend, and Jack Hayward.

The story of the Great Western is the stuff of myths and legends. Iconic names linked with it are also linked with 'masterpieces' or magnificence that still 'live' in the memory or have lasted through the years.

From its first inception and through the whole of its life, the GWR had to fight for its very existence. Financial crises, over-development, costly experiments, strikes, wars and government interference led it often to the brink of disaster, but it overcame these threats time and again until, in the end, matters were taken out of its own hands and transferred to those of the nation.

Bold and radical in enterprise, yet ultra-conservative in philosophy, the GWR was very much an 'institution' of its own making. Always greater than the sum of its parts and evoking many strong emotions, it demanded respect and loyalty, and won admiration and affection in return. Even now, in this 175th Inauguration Celebratory Year, many still claim the GWR to be, 'God's Wonderful Railway'.

THE COMPANY

It is often said that it was Isambard Kingdom Brunel, the iconic nineteenth-century engineer, who may have given the company its name – the Great Western

➤ *The GWR crest and coat of arms incorporating the shields of the cities of London (left) and Bristol (right).*

➤➤ *A wonderful depiction of the interior of Bristol's original GWR station showing the majestic width of the 7ft 0¼in broad gauge.*

Railway – but its nascent vision belonged to four businessmen of Bristol: George Jones, John Harford, Thomas Richard Guppy and William Tohill. These four gentlemen resolved to revive the interest in establishing a railway line between Bristol and London – first mooted in 1824 – and by the end of 1832 a committee of fifteen men, representing the various commercial and corporation interests of Bristol, was established. At their first public meeting in January 1833, it was agreed to provide funds for a preliminary survey and an estimation of the cost of such an undertaking. It was then that Brunel was taken on to carry out this work. Later that year the title of 'The Great Western Railway' was formally adopted in place of the previous 'Bristol and London Railroad' and a legend was born.

8

The route Brunel finally submitted to the Board would take the railroad from Bristol via Bath, Chippenham and to the north of what is now Swindon before going on to Reading, Maidenhead and finally on to London. Under the management of two committees, the Bristol and the London Committees, the first Great Western Bill was submitted to Parliament in 1834. It was carried by the Commons but defeated by the Lords on the grounds that 'the scheme offered insufficient security for the completion of the line'. Happily the second bill made better progress, and received the Royal Assent on 31 August 1835.

The GWR opened the first 22 miles of its new railway line from Paddington to Maidenhead to public traffic on 4 June 1838, and to Reading in March 1840. Work also started from the Bristol end and

eventually the two ends joined between Chippenham and Box.

Once this mainline was completed the GWR set out to 'capture' the West, making it 'Broad Gauge Country'. However, just a few short years down the line in 1845, they were literally stopped in their tracks. The 'Break of Gauge', where broad gauge

➤ 2-2-2 North Star, probably the most famous of the GWR's early engines, and also the first engine on the company's books. It had the distinction of working the first GWR passenger train on 31 May 1838 as the 'Director's Special'. Here it is shown outside the workshop having been modified from its original condition.

Did you know?

This monogram design was introduced in 1934 to replace all previous branding. The Great Western Railway's initials were used in several different ways, and most were less than complimentary!

'God's Wonderful Railway' – by its fans.

'Great Way Round' – this when some of its routes were rather circuitous.

'Goes When Ready' – a reference to the rather 'laid-back' approach of some of the smaller branch lines.

'God Wot Rot' – by those who favoured other companies!

'Greasy, Worn and Rusty' – regarding its condition after the Second World War!

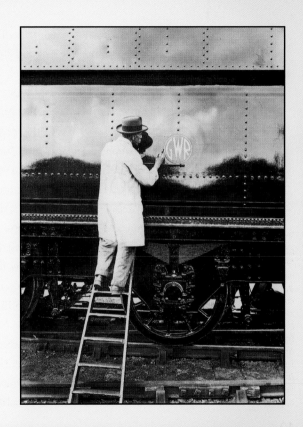

met narrow gauge, brought a dose of cold reality and the beginning of the end of the broad gauge.

1846 was a significant year that was to have a far-reaching consequences for the GWR. Firstly, it was the year that the Gauge Commissioners reported in favour of the narrow (now standard) 4ft 8½in gauge track which sounded the official death knell for Brunel's broad 7ft 0¼in gauge. Secondly, and more happily, it was the year that the GWR decided to completely build its own engines. Swindon Works had been established to repair and improve the rolling stock bought in by the company. They had started to part-build engines for freight work in 1845, but by 1846 the company badly needed their own engine to haul passenger trains that would outstrip their rivals. The Board ordered Daniel Gooch to build 'a colossal locomotive working with all speed'; he did so in record-breaking time. By continuously working day and night shifts, the men turned out the engine in just thirteen weeks – an incredible achievement when one remembers that it was still a time of man, muscle and blacksmithing skills. The aptly named *Great Western,* the first locomotive to be entirely built at Swindon Works, performed extremely well. It ran from Paddington to Exeter, a distance of 194 miles, in just three hours and twenty-eight minutes in June that year. It was described thus by the *Morning Herald*: 'Such a passenger train as *The Great Western* can propel at a maximum speed of 70 and an average of about 50 miles per hour, would require two or three narrow gauge locomotives to propel it at 38 or 40 miles per hour.'

Did you know?

SPECIAL NAMES

The GWR had several specially named passenger services, each with its own character and sense of glamour. Some of these were…

Broad gauge: 'Zulu', 'The Cornishman' and 'The Flying Dutchman' (the fastest train in the world for several decades).

Narrow gauge: 'The Bristolian', 'The Cambrian Coast Express', 'The Cheltenham Spa Express' (nicknamed 'The Cheltenham Flyer'), 'The Cornish Riviera Express' and 'The Torbay Express'.

The top picture shows one of William Dean's single driving wheel 'Rover' class locomotives c.1890 with some 'convertible' carriages mounted on broad gauge underframes. Below we see the 4-4-0 No.3433 City of Bath *locomotive built 1903 hauling the* Dutchman *near Slough now a standard gauge service.*

Flying Dutchman G.W.R.
NEAR SLOUGH.

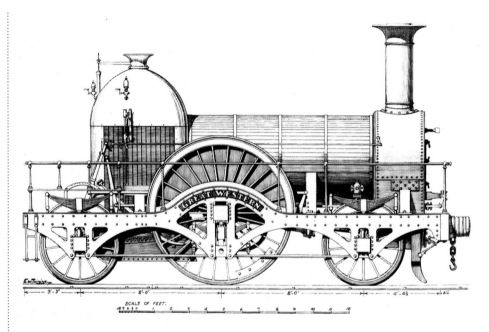

► *The first engine built entirely at Swindon Works, April 1846, was the 2-2-2* Great Western, *shown here from a drawing by E.W. Twining.*

►► *This photograph from around 1910 shows the interior of the new Wheel Shop or AW Shop, which was part of the new 'A' Shop; later relocated (1921) when the 'A' Shop extension opened. It is a fascinating record of the huge numbers and various diameters of wheels produced and employed by the GWR. (Paul William's Hooper Collection)*

Constructing a complete engine 'in-house' was to start a trend that would influence the philosophy of the GWR and shape company policy in the future. From now on, whenever possible, the GWR would always produce its own goods,

from engines, carriages, wagons, wheels and rails, its own tools, component parts, furniture, printing, even down to its own recycled soap!

In October 1864 the company said a reluctant 'goodbye' to Daniel Gooch, who resigned and took himself off to follow his own interests. The GWR had by this time expended a great deal of money not only on the development of Swindon Works but on other, less successful ventures, such as the atmospheric railway. The concept of the atmospheric railway was way ahead of the technology of its time. Despite Brunel's belief, rats, grease and inferior rubber could not be overcome, and the project was doomed to be an expensive failure. The directors were having a tough time in appeasing existing shareholders and attracting new investment. Realising the fragility of their future existence, they urged Gooch to return as Chairman to save them from financial ruin. Gooch took up his new post in November 1865 and used his business skills and strict economies to turn things around. To quote MacDermott, he was able to 'establish [the GWR's] fortunes on a firm basis of prosperity.'

The GWR stood out from other railways principally because of its broad gauge, but in some respects it was this that stymied its development. By the 1880s they were rather in the doldrums, not helped by the ongoing effects of the Great Depression. The *first* Great Depression came much earlier than the 1930s and lasted longer – from 1873–1896 – with heavy and sustained general unemployment, widespread gloom in the business world and a particular lack of confidence with regard to railway

◄ *Known locally as 'the Works' Mad Rush', workers leave for home via the Main Tunnel Entrance in London Street. (Paul William's Hooper Collection)*

investments. It was a tough time as the company made stringent cuts all over the system. Yet, extraordinarily through this difficult period, Swindon Works continued to expand. By 1890 the number employed in the Works had risen to 9,471 and it had become, to quote the company's magazine of November that year, 'certainly the largest centre of railway industry in England, and probably in the world', a proud boast that would be repeated over many decades.

The 'laying-to-rest' of the broad gauge in May 1892 brought a new era to the GWR and the years between 1895 and

Early view of Swindon Works and Railway Village, 1849. (Jack Hayward Collection)

1914 are often referred to as 'the Glorious Years', 'the Golden Age' or 'the reign of George Jackson Churchward' and his incredible machines. It was an era that was to establish Churchward's reputation as an outstanding locomotive engineer that lives on to this day. It was the era that brought alive again the 'romance' of the GWR and put the 'Great' back into Great Western. The 'Golden Age' established the GWR as the 'Holiday Line' as they opened up the now standard gauge to the West Country, seducing new customers with the Cornish Riviera.

The 'Golden Days' led into some of the 'Darkest Days' for the company, country and the world. On 4 August 1914 England made its declaration of war on Germany. The next day, under Section 16 of the Regulation of the Forces Act 1871, the British Government announced its intention to take over control of the railroads in Great Britain. Whilst the railways would still run under the administration of the Executive Committee of Railway Managers, the priorities of the War Office for the movement of troops, stores and food supplies, were paramount. All railway companies were expected to do

◄ The GWR used many artists and many styles of artwork to sell their 'Holiday Line', especially those 'Bound for the West' and the exciting 'Cornish Riviera'. (David Hyde Collection)

 SPEED TO THE WEST
CORNWALL DEVON SOMERSET WALES

◀◀ *The mighty 4-6-0 'King' class locomotive was designed to work the heavily loaded express trains on the West Country route as far as Plymouth. This poster, first issued in the late 1930s, also shows the carriages then in use on the 'Cornish Riviera Express'. (David Hyde Collection)*

◀ *The out-shopping of each new locomotive at Swindon Works was a time of excitement and a moment of enormous pride to those who had worked on her, especially the men of the Erecting Shop.*

➤ *Miss George was the GWR's first female ticket collector, taken on during the First World War.*

➤➤ *Newly completed Ambulance Ward Car ready for delivery to active service in the war effort of the First World War.*

their duty and the GWR did so. The number of items that it carried in support of the war effort is staggering: 376,787 officers and men, 33,101 horses, 355 guns and limbers, 264 ammunitions wagons, 2,034 bicycles, 180 motorcycles, 1,492 four-wheel wagons and 803 two-wheel wagons, all in 846 special trains (numbers taken from the GWR's *Magazine*).

The First World War highlighted the folly of running the railway system as it had been previously. In the rationalisation that followed, the Railways Act of 1921 divided some 180 separate organisations into four main groups; the London North Eastern Railway (LNER), the London Midland Scottish Railway (LMS), the Southern Railway and the GWR. These then became known and loved, and live on in memory as 'The Big Four'. On 1 January

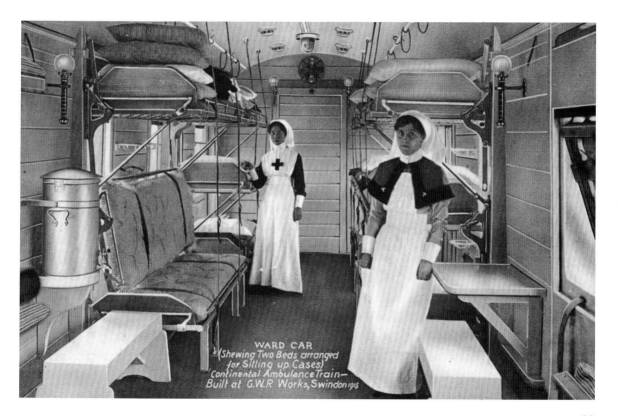

WARD CAR
(Shewing Two Beds arranged
for Sitting up Cases)
Continental Ambulance Train—
Built at G.W.R Works, Swindon 1915

23

➤ *Two iconic GWR names recognised in the 'Castle' class. (Bob Townsend Photographs)*

➤➤ *The GWR 4073 or 'Castle' class entered into service in 1923. This is an early depiction of the famous and ever popular* Pendennis Castle, *seen here with a short-sided tender. Built in the first batch of ten, she was outshipped from Swindon Works in February 1924 and worked out of Old Oak Common. In later life she spent some time working 'down under' in Australia but is now part of the Great Western Society locomotive collection at Didcot Railway Centre.*

1923 the Great Western Railway was the only company to survive intact and in its original form, to keep its name and its management structure, thus perpetuating its proud traditions and 'difference' from other railways. The *esprit de coeur* that was an almost tangible element in the make-up of the GWR, beat stronger still!

This new era started well, with the introduction of what became one of the GWR's most famous locomotive classes, and 'Castles' became the word on everyone's lips.

The General Strike of 1926 brought conversation of a different nature and the country to a virtual standstill. From 3–12

May millions of men and women stood together in workers' solidarity. The GWR were stunned and stung by how many of their employees joined the action. After the return to work, the talk was of the vindictiveness of the GWR management. Many strikers were not taken back and every participant's work records were marked. It took a long-time for the wounds to heal… on both sides! The arrival of the colossal 'King' class, the most famous being the *King George V* No.6000, built in 1927, helped change the talk to happier things, although just for a short time!

The tough, depressed years of the 1930s were, paradoxically, also the years of 'speed and glamour' for the GWR. In 1933 the GWR did not just 'fly' along the rails, it also flew through the air with their inauguration of the Railway Air Service.

The difficult times of cutbacks, lay-offs and short-time working, were all forgotten in 1935 when the company's centenary was celebrated with high spirits. One notable celebration was the making of an educational 'sound film' called *The Romance of a Railway*, depicting the birth, early history and some of the various contemporary aspects of the company. A replica of the broad gauge engine *North Star* was used and members of the GWR (London) Operatic Society took part.

The first edition of Heath Robinson cartoons of railway life, *Railway Ribaldry*, was produced along with a special centenary *Holiday Haunts* guide. To commemorate the Bristol association with the company, a luncheon was held on inauguration day in the Great Hall of Bristol University and a new-named

◀ As part of its centenery celebrations, the GWR commissioned a painting from which they created a special poster entitled '100 years of Progress 1835–1935' showing a state-of-the-art King class locomotive hauling 'chocolate and cream' carriages of the 'Torbay Express', speeding along the Devon coastline. (David Hyde Collection)

100 YEARS OF PROGRESS
1835 — 1935

GWR

passenger service – 'The Bristolian' – was introduced as a high-speed non-stop service between London and Bristol. In October a magnificent banquet was held in London. Two new centre-corridor trains were built and formed the 'Cornish Riviera Express' service. They were constructed with vestibules and large windows rather than individual doors and small windows and given special upholstery.

The annual report for 1935 indicated a year of 'steady progress and consolidation'. It also gives us an indication of the breadth of the company at that time. There were reports from the Traffic Department (including Railway Air Services); Goods;

Chief Mechanical Engineer's: Engineering; Signals; Solicitor's & Legal and Surveyor's & Estates Departments, as well as from Hotels & Refreshments Rooms; Stores; Stationery & Printing; Docks and Road Transport too.

Just when things really seemed to be getting better for the company and the

THE NEW SALOON FOR OCEAN TRAFFIC.

◄▲ *(David Hyde Collection)*

▼ Using GWR's house removal services, the householder got a special rate for their rail journey. This evocative if posed scene took place in Acton, London, 1933. (David Hyde Collection)

The GWR had its own Home Guard from July 1940. Here they are marching alongside the J1 Iron Foundry in Swindon Works, 1941.

➤ *On the basis of releasing men for the Services and for the duration of the war only, war-recruited women did previously 'men-only' jobs all over the railways in order to keep them running.*

➤➤ *A line-up of some of the jobs women did on the GWR during the Second World War.*

country, war was declared once again. The Second World War hammered the railways. It hammered the people of Britain too. No longer was war fought 'abroad', as new technology brought it to one's own home.

Huge numbers were recruited into the war effort and large numbers of women took their place alongside railwaymen to produce armaments in railway workshops and do 'proper' railway work in order to keep Britain's railways running. At the

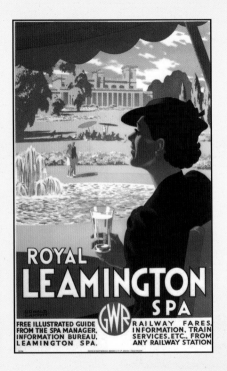

▲▶ (Great Western Trust Collection)

Did you know?

PUBLICITY

The GWR were excellent publicists, using many techniques modern-day marketing agencies would be proud of. It had a 'tag' line: *'Go Great Western'*. Branding itself 'The Holiday Line', it created the concept of the 'Cornish Riviera' and used many artists to design eye-catching posters to lure passengers there.

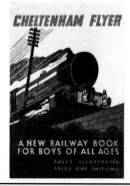

A UNIQUE SET OF BOOKS

The GWR produced a series of eight much-loved books. The first book in 1923, *The 10.30 Limited*, was such a success that *Caerphilly Castle: A Book of Railway Locomotives For Boys of All Ages* followed in 1924, and that famous phrase was born – 'books for boys of all ages'. These titles were followed by *Twixt Rail and Sea*, *The 'King' of Railway Locomotives*, *Cheltenham Flyer*, *Track Topics*, *Loco's of the Royal Road* and *Brunel and After*.

In 1925 Pendennis Castle *was loaned to the LNER for comparative trials with Sir Nigel Gresley's new 4-6-0 locomotives. Though smaller in size,* Pendennis Castle *outperformed her rivals sending Gresley back to the drawing board before eventually developing his famous A4 class. The whole episode was a veritable triumph for Swindon design. The engine, seen here during the trial pulling an immense train, which it handled most competently, is now preserved by the Great Western Society at Didcot. (Brian Arman Collection)*

end of the Second World War the GWR, a reluctant female recruiter the first time around, had some 16,000 railwaywomen and were proud of the fact too.

At the end of the war the country said 'goodbye' to the war-recruited women as they went back to their homes. A few years later the country said 'goodbye' to privately owned railway companies. When the Transport Act of 1947 came into effect on 1 January 1948, nationalising all British railways, the control of the Great Western Railway passed to the British Transport Commission and the Great Western Railway Company, which had been in existence for 112 years, was no more.

For those new to the world of railways, the term 'gauge' means the distance between the inside edges of the running rails. The history of the 'gauges' on British railways would probably have been straightforward (and less interesting) had it not been for the broad gauge, instead of which its history has a special *piquance* that still resonates today.

The story of the gauges actually begins with the problems experienced with the early rails or track. Whilst it is George Stephenson whose name is popularly associated with what the GWR called the 'narrow' and the rest called the 'standard' gauge, its origins lie more with William Jessop. Originally the 'railroads' laid to carry coal from the colliery to the canals or depots were constructed to a width to allow the horses that hauled the coal wagons to walk between the rails. The materials used to construct the rails were always unsatisfactory and constantly undergoing redevelopment. When Jessop designed his flanged iron wagon wheels and his smooth iron-edge rails in 1789, he made the radical decision to run the wheels on the inside of the edge-rails as this would help keep the wheels in position on the axles. This made

▼ Vulcan *was one of the first two engines received (25 November 1837) by the GWR and the first to be tried in steam. By 1846 it had been altered from a tender engine to how we see it here, a 2-2-2 back tank retaining the 8ft driving wheels but with 4ft carrying wheels.*

➤ 'Smile for the camera!' A local track gang carrying out general maintenance work in a rare picture of a broad gauge scene (around 1886) at Box Station (on the right) with its splendid Brunellian 'chimney pots'. Note the impressive gas lamps on the 'up' platform, despite its basic facilities. In the background can be seen the portal of Box Middle Tunnel and on right the narrow gauge pilot engine (1076 class).

➤➤ *Caesar class 0-6-0* Dido *built at Swindon Works in June 1851, a typical early broad gauge goods locomotive. (Most pictures in this chapter from Brian Arman Collection)*

the 'new' gauge 5ft minus the width of his two rails, giving a gauge of 4ft 8in.

George Stephenson was a self-taught, practical man. His knowledge and expertise came from his 'hands-on' experience gained in different jobs at the various collieries he had worked in. When he hand-built his first locomotive *Blucher* to

➤ *South Devon Railway*
Buffalo class 0-6-0
Dragon *as GWR 2164*
seen with attendant staff
outside Launceston shed,
c.1890.

haul wagons for Killingworth Colliery in 1813, he sensibly followed the gauge of 4ft 8in which was already in use there. He adopted this gauge again when building his first railway, the historic Stockton and Darlington Railway, and subsequently the Liverpool and Manchester, and so embedded it with his name forever.

By the coming of the GWR this 'narrow' gauge had spread over the northern and south-eastern parts of the country, not least because it was usually specified (and after 1846 definitely specified) by a clause in the Acts authorising construction of new railways. Somewhere along the line a half an inch was added (to allow expansion), taking the gauge to 4ft 8½in and it was this gauge that was used thereafter and is now accepted as the 'standard' gauge.

Somehow (some say as a result of Brunel's fierce negotiations) this gauge clause had been omitted from the 1835 Great Western Railway Act, which left Brunel with a free hand to do what he normally did – his-own thing! Ironically the 1834 Bill had contained this gauge specification and had it been granted the broad gauge would never have happened; an industrial endeavour of epic proportions, and a fevered debate that has lasted centuries, would never have come about.

Brunel was of a different calibre to Stephenson. He was not a 'follower', nor an 'adopter'. He was an inventor. He was passionate about his gauge; time and again he argued in its favour and defence. Firstly he convinced the GWR directors in 1835 and in 1839 he had to persuade the anxious shareholders to stay the course. Later in

41

1845 he had to defend it to the Gauge Commission! The vision behind the 7ft 0¼in (2.2m) gauge was that Brunel never intended to build just for his time. He saw the need to build for the volume and mass of the transport of the future. His gauge, he argued, would enable trains to travel faster, more comfortably, carry more passengers more economically and be safer, especially when travelling at speeds around curves, and now, in this modern day, we know him to be right. Being right, however, did not make it any easier, for, in truth, Brunel arrived on the scene a little too late, and the area that the GWR covered with broad gauge was a little too little, never getting north of Wolverhampton. Because of this, the odds were always stacked against them.

Inevitably there came a 'crunch-time' when broad gauge met the narrow gauge of another company. When it did, it set in motion a hue and cry that reverberated throughout the country, taken up by the press and protagonists and even painters! The 'Break of Gauge' hullabaloo was highlighted at Gloucester where the broad gauge of the Bristol & Gloucester met the narrow gauge of the Birmingham & Gloucester line. The situation created havoc for passengers, goods and animals that needed to travel onwards, requiring everyone and everything to be taken off one train and transferred onto the other (in both directions!), whilst for those travelling by the GWR to Paddington, via Swindon or South Wales, it also entailed a change of station too! For the travelling public it was, 'unpleasant in the night time and in cold weather, and highly inconvenient to mothers with families, and to the lame

◄◄ Contemporary depiction of the 'Break of Gauge' at Gloucester, playing up the 'tearing, swearing, de'il-may-caring' chaos.

➤ *Locomotive No.57 was the first narrow gauge engine built at Swindon in May 1855. It was withdrawn in 1912 and is seen here much rebuilt in its final condition.*

and blind', and for station staff it brought to them a 'loss of direction, pilferage and detention of hours'. Such was the clamour that in 1845 a Gauge Commission was set up to look into the matter with George Airy, Astronomer Royal, Sir Frederick Smith and Professor Peter Barlow as Commissioners.

The 'Battle of the Gauges' was fiercely fought on both sides. Many 'ingenious arguments, much wit, some ill-humour and spirit of partisanship of the bitterest nature' were exhibited on all sides. During a series of interviews between August and December 1845, the commission interrogated forty-seven persons made up of 'railway engineers, engine makers, railway managers, carriers, miners, and railway contractors', and even the military! Not all supported either of the disputed gauges. Arguments were put forward for a variety of gauges, including 5ft 3in and 6ft.[1] A trial was ordered whereby two narrow gauge engines were chosen for comparison with the broad gauge engine *Ixion* of Gooch's 'Firefly' Class. Despite the superior performance of *Ixion*, and despite admitting the technical superiority and potential of Brunel's ideas, the commission finally found in favour of the narrow gauge in 1846. This finding was to have a far-reaching effect on the GWR and its finances, as, once the commission had declared for the now 'standard' gauge, a full conversion was inevitable.

The GWR had acquired narrow gauge lines in 1850 and needed to link them to the rest of the system. It had introduced 'mixed' gauge (able to take narrow and broad gauge) by way of a 'narrow gauge third rail' on their lines as early as 1852, with the 66-mile mixed gauge route between Oxford and Birmingham. They had started constructing narrow gauge engines at Swindon Works in the mid-1850s, this despite not having narrow gauge laid to Swindon, which created something of a delivery problem! Yet, it still must have felt like an insult when mixed gauge eventually arrived at Paddington in October 1861. It would only get worse. 1868 was the year of the first broad gauge conversion *to* standard gauge between Princes Risborough and Aylesbury, and 1869 saw the first large-scale conversion.

➤ Lord of the Isles, *the most famous of the 4-2-2 'Iron Duke' class, probably because of its history of being exhibited – firstly at the Great Exhibition of 1851 and after withdrawal from service in 1884 at Edinburgh in 1890, Chicago in 1893 and finally Earl's Court in 1897.*

This is one of the very earliest railway photographs, taken at Swindon Works around 1852, with St Mark's Church in the background. It was probably taken after repair work to the engine carried out after the accident which occurred on its first outing as a 'special' on the opening of the broad gauge route to Birmingham.

In 1866 Gooch, by then the Chairman of the company, had reported to shareholders that:

There is no doubt it has become necessary for us to look the matter of the narrow gauge fairly in the face. We have had within the past few days a memorial signed by nearly every firm of any standing in South Wales wishing that the narrow gauge might be carried out in their district. It is also pressing upon us in many other districts.

Despite this, and constrained by financial difficulties, the 'mix and match' approach continued. The GWR were continually absorbing and amalgamating other broad gauge lines, such as the Bristol & Exeter, the South Devon, the Cornwall and West Cornwall railways. Broad gauge was still being laid as late as 1877 on the St Erth to St Ives branch line, pure broad gauge engines were still being built at Swindon – the *Prometheus, Great Western* and *Tornado* in April, May and July 1888 respectively – and a new broad gauge express, the 'Cornishman' was actually introduced in 1890. Broad gauge was doing well in GWR territory, but it could not last!

Happily, Gooch had done his new job well and when he died in October 1889, the company had the means to tackle the broad gauge problem. They were galvanised into action. In January 1890 William Dean, Locomotive Superintendent, prepared an estimate of the costings for converting the whole of the broad gauge locomotive, carriage and wagon stock to 'narrow' gauge (the GWR persisted in

The Great Western, one of the three last broad gauge engines, was built in May 1888 and the last to be named, photographed at Didcot Station around 1890. Known unofficially as the 'Rover' class, Great Western had a working life of just four years. It hauled one of the last broad gauge expresses, the 10.15 a.m. departure from Paddington to Penzance, as far as Bristol.

referring to it as 'narrow' gauge even at this late stage). The net amount, he quoted, after allowing for the value of old material, was: Locomotive Stock – £107,040; Coaching & Merchandise Stock – £255,320; Total – £362,360.

Dean suggested that in respect of locomotive stock, some '£107,040 could be charged to Revenue in the ordinary course of Renewals in the four half-years ending June & December 1890 and 1891', whilst the same could be done for Coaching & Merchandise to the sum of £165,320, leaving only '£90,000 in suspense to which should be added an amount of say £10,000 representing the net cost of temporary sidings [at Swindon Works] which would be required to accommodate the stock during the time of conversion.'

May 1892 was the final reckoning. On Friday 20 May 1892, at 5 p.m., the very last broad gauge passenger train left Paddington for Plymouth behind the Iron Duke class 4-2-2 engine *Bulkeley*. It also hauled the last 'up' broad gauge train as it returned with the mail early on Saturday morning. The last miles of broad gauge track to be lifted were the main line between Exeter and Truro and several branches, a total of 171 miles. It presented special problems for much of it was single track and there were no alternative routes. The mammoth task was carried out over just one weekend, Saturday 21 and Sunday 22 May. On Thursday 19 May some 4,200 company men had arrived from different parts of the system, bringing with them tents, straw, food and tools, ready for the fateful job. They pitched up all down the track. A lot of preparatory work had already been done, with marking out and pre-oiling, but it was still an incredible feat of engineering accomplished with picks, shovels and saws, in an awesome thirty-one hours. As the *Railway Gazette* GWR Centenary issue expressed it, 'a triumph of organisation and engineering skill reflecting the highest credit on all concerned.' Amazingly, just as the GWR had ordered, the first narrow gauge 'Cornishman' left Penzance at its usual time Monday morning and arrived four minutes early at Paddington! But this was a demonstration only. After this, sanity came to the workings and trains obeyed local speed restrictions until the track had properly settled!

➤ GWR dignitaries and onlookers say 'goodbye' to the last broad gauge 'Cornishman' passenger express at 10.15 a.m. on 20 May 1892. It was worked by the Great Western from Paddington as far as Bristol.

The impact of all this on the Swindon Works was huge. It became a 'conversion' shop, what the GWR *Magazine* more accurately called 'the Mortuary'! The defunct stock was amassed in sidings and in the Concentration Yard (this was the site of the future 'A' Shop and not the 'Con' Yard of later years). Many new men were taken on to cope with the extra work. The company, knowing that this change was inevitable, had been prepared and constructed a large proportion of new locomotives and some of the carriage and wagon stock as 'convertibles', and these were speedily turned around and put back into service. In July 1892 Dean wrote to the Board that there were 196 Engines, 347 Carriages, 242 Pass & Brake Vans, Horse Boxes & Carriage Trucks, 3,302 Goods Wagons & Vans of these 69 Engines, 26 Carriages, 105 Pass Vans Horse Boxes &

Carriage Trucks and about 2,200 Goods Wagons & Vans required renewal and have been replaced by new Narrow Gauge stock. 32 Engines, 266 Carriages, 85 Pass Vans Horse Boxes & Carriage Trucks and 755 Goods Wagons & Vans have been converted to Narrow Gauge and the conversion of the

▲ *'Rover' class 4-2-2 Dragon at Taunton, replaced Great Western at Bristol and worked the final 'Cornishman' as far as Newton Abbott on 20 May 1892.*

51

➤ Broad gauge wagons stacked up in the specially constructed sidings at Swindon Works, now occupied by the Oasis Leisure Centre!

➤➤ Broad gauge carriages awaiting their fate in 'the BG Mortuary', 1892.

remainder is being proceeded with as rapidly as possible.

It was a massive undertaking. A small paragraph in a letter from Dean to the Board on 17 July 1893 states, 'The conversion of the broad gauge stock remaining on hand at the commencement of the present year has now been completed'. The job was done. Broad gauge had been confined to history.

NOTES

1   Information from the Commission's full text of 'Gauge Evidence – The history & prospects of the railway system'.

◀◀ *The end of an era. Broad gauge engines of different types assembled in the sidings at Swindon Works. From left to right:* Goat, Owl, Prince *and* Leopard. *The first three were actually converted to standard gauge.*

◀ *A well-known picture of a broad gauge engine steaming through the infamous Sonning Cutting (scene of a dreadful accident due to land-slippage on Christmas Eve 1841, where nine people died and several were badly injured), pulling 'convertible' carriages during the very last days of the broad gauge.*

ISAMBARD KINGDOM BRUNEL

Brunel was a man of enormous vision and boldness, bold enough to take risks, even to putting his own money into his projects, and his own life on the line. He went from 'building castles in the air' (his words) to building world heritage monuments. Born in Portsmouth and educated in Paris, he did his 'work experience' in the workshops of watchmaker Louis Breguet and then machine-tool craftsman Henry Maudslay. Isambard found his engineering feet working with his father Marc, a French engineer, on the Thames Tunnel. The passion and drive he brought to this project set the tone and pace that was to determine his work pattern for the rest of his life. It is said that this, along with his passion for smoking cigars, eventually lead to his early death at fifty-three years of age.

> *Isambard Kingdom Brunel, Second Greatest Britain of All Time, born in Portsmouth, 9 April 1806; died in London, 15 September 1859. He is shown standing before some of his great works – the Royal Albert Bridge, Box Tunnel and the broad gauge railtrack. (Painting by J.E. Grigson GRA)*

Although the range of Brunel's engineering feats is incredibly wide, encompassing the first transatlantic steam-powered liners, the docks at Bristol basin and guns and hospitals in the Crimea in aid of the British war effort, it is with the Great Western Railway that his name is umbilically linked. The names Isambard Kingdom Brunel and the Great Western Railway are synonymous; one is not complete without the other! With the GWR he will be best remembered for his broad gauge, marvellous mathematical bridges, mesmerising tunnels and his great ships.

The design and construction of the great SS *Great Western*, *Great Britain* and *Great Eastern* took up much of Brunel's later career. These brought him a great deal of worry and it was shortly after the launch of the *Great Eastern*, and the opening of the incredible Royal Albert Bridge, that he died.

Despite his passion for work, Brunel was apparently indifferent to amassing a fortune and left an estate of only £90,000. In his stove-pipe hat and adopting a bravado stance, he has become an iconic figure of the Victorian Industrial Revolution and captured the imagination of the people of the twenty-first century. In 2002, he was voted 'The Second Greatest Britain of All Time'.

THE COMPANY'S MEN

Gooch, Armstrong, Dean and Churchward were all 'company men' in the strongest sense of the term. Sir Daniel Gooch not only gave the company sound and splendid engines, he also used his business acumen for his own and the company's good. Armstrong looked after the company's

interests whilst keeping the welfare of the working men close to his heart. It is William Dean who is most remembered for being the one who bore the brunt of the broad gauge conversion but it was his successor, George Jackson Churchward, who heralded the truly golden years of GWR locomotives.

DANIEL GOOCH

Daniel Gooch, later Sir Daniel Gooch, a superb locomotive engineer, was also one of the new 'breed' of 'managers' to emerge through the Industrial Revolution. A self-made man with an instinct for business and for being in the right place at the right time, he amassed a substantial personal fortune. Gooch had trained in engineering at some notable companies, so he had good credentials when he wrote what has to be the most famous railway 'application letter' ever to Brunel:

Dear Sir

I have just been informed that it is your intention to erect an Engine Manufactory at or near Bristol and that you wish to engage a person as manager. I take the earliest opportunity of offering my services for the situation… I am anxious to engage Myself to some company where I have the management of the building of Engines… I trust you approve of my application. I shall be glad to hear from you stating the Salary and any other information you may think necessary.

Gooch's appointment on 18 August 1837 when still not quite twenty-one years old would bring benefits to the GWR many times over; not just with his joint decision on the site of Swindon Works, not just with his engines but, more importantly, with his saving of the company from bankruptcy some thirty years later. (The GWR expressed their thanks by rewarding him £5,000 – what we would today call 'a bonus'.)

In September 1840 Gooch wrote his second famous letter to Brunel regarding the site of the proposed 'engine establishment'. The consequence of this letter was the creation of a railway town – Swindon – and a railway works of world repute, that Gooch was to nourish and protect throughout his time with the GWR. It was this attachment that prompted him to write his third famous letter in November 1847. Touched by the plight of the laid-off men in Swindon and by the valiant efforts of those who were still in work to support them, Gooch wrote

Sir Daniel Gooch (born in Bedlington, Northumberland, 24 August 1816; died in Clewer, Windsor, 15 October 1889). He was the Locomotive Superintendent from August 1837–October 1864 and Chairman from November 1865–October 1889.

➤ *Joseph Armstrong (born in Bewcastle, Cumberland, 21 September 1816; died on 5 June 1877 in Matlock, Bath). He was Locomotive Superintendent from January 1864 but he became the first Locomotive, Carriage & Wagon Superintendent from 1866–June 1877.*

to the company requesting permission to provide some medical assistance to the men. The GWR, recognising the benefits to the company, agreed and the GWR Medical Fund Society came into being. No one could have guessed at its far-reaching outcomes, for it was to become a role model for the new NHS, which brought the benefits that we all share in today.

The first locomotive built to Gooch's design was the 2-2-2 *Firefly* which raised the benchmark in engine design. In 1846 he produced the superlative *Great Western*, prototype of the Iron Duke class 4-2-2, and the GWR's reputation for good looks and speed began.

Gooch resigned in September 1864 to pursue his interest in laying the first transatlantic cable, using the SS *Great Eastern* (which earned him a Baronetcy). He became a Conservative MP for Cricklade, the constituency that then included Swindon, the following year, but he could not turn his back on the company that made him in their hour of need and in November 1865 he returned as Chairman, a post he still held when he died in October 1889, aged seventy-three. Gooch had held a strong affection for the broad gauge, so it is fitting that he should not have had to see its inglorious demise.

JOSEPH ARMSTRONG

Joseph Armstrong must have found it a very daunting task to step into Gooch's shoes, but in thirteen short years he was to make his own strong mark on the GWR at Swindon Works and especially on its railway community. A man who lead from the front, he took a leading role in the establishment and development of many of New Swindon's institutions.

Unlike Gooch, Joseph Armstrong took some time to work his way up to his lofty final position at the age of forty-eight. He too had worked with notable names and places in the engineering world. Starting out as a driver on the Liverpool & Manchester Railway, he was foreman of the running shed of the Hull & Selby Railway and then the Locomotive Superintendent of the Shrewsbury & Chester Railway. He came to the GWR by 'accident' upon the amalgamation of that railway and the Shrewsbury & Birmingham lines (where he had been in control of their combined stock) with the GWR. In 1854 he became Gooch's assistant and Northern Division Superintendent at Wolverhampton Works. Upon Gooch's resignation, Armstrong succeeded him as Locomotive

➤➤ *William Dean oversaw the last of broad gauge production. The 8ft single* Great Western *(1888) was one of the last three. (Great Western Trust Collection)*

Superintendent at Swindon. He used his engineering skills to work with broad and narrow gauge locomotives and produced the first batch of GWR 'convertibles' in 1876.

In 1866 Gooch had agreed the building of the new Carriage & Wagon Works at Swindon and Armstrong became the first Superintendent of both Locomotive *and* Carriage & Wagon Works. He managed the huge expansion at Swindon and, surprisingly, introduced a new workshop for female workers in 1874. This radical thinking was needed to overcome recruitment problems regarding skilled men.

Joseph Armstrong worked hard for the men in his charge, some say too hard, for this eventually lead to his death. He was so admired that on his death an RNLI lifeboat *Joseph Armstrong*, based at Cadgwith in Cornwall, was dedicated in his memory by the people of New Swindon.

WILLIAM DEAN

William Dean was a well-educated boy when, aged fifteen years, he was apprenticed to Joseph Armstrong at the GWR's Wolverhampton Stafford Road Works in 1855. Such was the excellence he showed, he was made Armstrong's chief assistant as soon as he completed his eight year apprenticeship, aged just twenty-four. When Armstrong moved to Swindon and his brother George took over, Dean became the Stafford Road Works' manager. In 1868 Armstrong brought Dean to Swindon to be his chief assistant and and when Joseph died in his post, Dean was his natural successor.

Whilst Dean designed the 'Duke' and the 'Bulldog' classes and is well known for

63

➤ William Dean (born in London, 8 January 1840; died in Folkestone, 4 September 1905). He was the Locomotive, Carriage & Wagon Superintendent from June 1877–June 1902.

the 'Dean's Goods' workhorses, it is for his work with carriages that he is more likely to be remembered. Dean ushered in a new era of passenger comfort that was to give us that still well-loved institution, 'the corridor train'. He introduced the first lavatories, electric lights and heating to coaches, and, not forgetting those hard-working men driving the train, he introduced cabs for drivers.

Many of Dean's designs included batches of 'convertibles' ready for the inevitable conversion of the broad gauge, and he spent his whole time in office, twenty-five years in total, dealing with the effects of the broad gauge problem, right through to its final demise. Dogged by ill-health in the last years of his working life, he retired to Folkestone to a house bought for him by the GWR and died three years later.

GEORGE JACKSON CHURCHWARD

George Jackson Churchward started his railway life aged sixteen, working under the Locomotive, Carriage & Wagon Superintendent of the broad gauge South Devon Railway at Newton Abbot. When the SDR was absorbed by the GWR in 1878, he was transferred to Swindon Works' Drawing Office, working as a draughtsman, where his potential was soon recognised. Churchward had a sound 'Works' training', first as Assistant Carriage Works Manager, then Manager (1882–85) before moving over and becoming Locomotive Works Manager from 1886. He then became Assistant to William Dean in 1892, before becoming solely responsible as Locomotive, Carriage & Wagon Superintendent in 1902. However, in truth, he had been 'in charge' some

George Jackson Churchward CBE (born in Stoke Gabriel, Devon, 31 January 1857; died on 19 December 1933). He was made the Locomotive, Carriage & Wagon Superintendent in June 1902. His title was then altered and he became the first Chief Mechanical Engineer in 1916, a position he held until December 1921.

years before this because of Dean's increasingly frail health.

Once 'in post', Churchward began his engineering 'reformation', starting with the boiler. Influenced by locomotive practice in the USA and after some experimentation, he came up with his now famous tapered boiler. Churchward's era produced the revolutionary 'Saint' Class, the 'City', 'Star' and 'County' classes and the *Great Bear*. In all of this, 'standardisation' in production became a Churchwardian byword. His works, too many to mention them all, have inspired large numbers of books.

Churchward retired in 1922. He was tragically killed whilst crossing the lines on the misty morning of 19 December 1933. His funeral on 22 December brought Swindon to a standstill as thousands lined the streets.

CHARLES BENJAMIN COLLETT

Reared within sight of GWR's Paddington Station, Collett was twenty-two years old when he joined the Swindon drawing office as a junior draughtsman. Within five years he was appointed to the post of Assistant to the Chief Draughtsman. In June 1900 he was made the Assistant Manager at Swindon Locomotive Works and shortly after became the Works Manager. Appointed Deputy Chief Mechanical Engineer in May 1919, his path to Chief Mechanical Engineer after Churchward was assured.

Collett was probably the least charismatic of all the GWR's 'Great Men'. He was also probably the least 'company' man, known for his intolerance of pomposity, particularly that of the directors. Widowed early, he remained aloof from any social

◄ *Charles Benjamin Collettt OBE (born in London, 10 September 1871; died in Wimbledon, 5 April 1952). He was the Chief Mechanical Engineer from 1922–1941 and was awarded the OBE for his work during the First World War.*

activities but was noted for his sound manufacturing understanding and quiet management skills, exercising powerful authority at Paddington.

It is often said that Collett merely expanded on Churchward's standard machines, but in truth and in fairness, Collett improved the design and the manufacturing techniques so that the originals were turned into precision machines, and thus he was responsible for the GWR's flagships, the 'Castles' and 'Kings'.

FREDERICK W. HAWKSWORTH

A quiet, private man, few words have been written on Hawksworth. A Swindon born and bred man, he was apprenticed to the GWR in 1898, became a draughtsman in 1905 and assistant to Collett in 1932. Hawksworth took up the post of Chief Mechanical Engineer in the middle of the Second World War and had to accommodate production to the ever-growing war demands. Surprisingly, he, unlike Collett before him, was happy to introduce war-recruited women into the Swindon workshops to do men's railway work. In 1946 he introduced the gas-turbine electric loco on the GWR express passenger trains.

◀ *Frederick W. Hawksworth (born in Swindon, 10 February 1884; died in Swindon, 13 July 1976). He was the last GWR Chief Mechanical Engineer, serving between 1941–1947 (1949).*

➤ Looking splendid in colour, Actaeon, one of Gooch's notable 'Firefly' class built by Nasmyth, Gaskell & Co. and delivered to the GWR in December 1841. On the right of the picture can be seen an early safety device, a visual indicator of how the points were set.

➤➤ 'Pacific' 111 Great Bear, one of Churchward's 'iconic' engines. (Jack Hayward Collection)

71

The "King" of Railway L[...]

G.W.R. EXPRESS PASSENGER LOCOMOTIVE "K[...]

"King George V" is the first of the Great Western Railway Company's "King" class of locomotives, th[...]

Designed and produced by Mr. C. B. Collett, C.B.E., Chief Mechanical Engineer of the Great Western [...]

Cylinders (four)—Diameter	16¼ in.	
Piston Stroke ..	28 in.	
Heating Surface total	2,514 sq. ft.	
Grate Area	34.3 sq. ft.	

Boiler Pressure	250 lb. per sq. in[...]
Barrel length	16 ft.
Barrel diameter (outside)	6 ft. and 5 ft. 6¼ [...]
Firebox length (outside)	11 ft. 6 in.
Tractive Effort at 85 per cent. B.P.	40,300 lb.

➤ (David Hyde Collection)

otives

GREAT WESTERN

ORGE V"

erful passenger train engines in Great Britain.
he Company's Locomotive Works at Swindon.

Wheels—Bogie, diameter ..   ..   3 ft.
              Coupled ..   ..   ..   6 ft. 6 in.
Water Capacity of Tender ..   ..   4,000 gallons
Weight of Engine and Tender (in working order) 135 tons 14 cwt.

RECYCLE

The GWR were into recycling before we knew what it was to be 'green'. They recycled old wagons into 'good and useful timber', then 'inferior wood for furnaces' and lastly 'old timber' and 'refuse' which was cut up and sold as firewood to Swindon Works' employees.

Timber from old carriages was sold on too. Carriage step-boards were often used in gardens and allotments for edging and net-rack poles were sold in bundles of a dozen for trellis work or bean-stick poles.

➤ The GWR tackled the 'threat' of motorised transport head on by creating its own road transport department. Some of these services had already existed under 'horse-power' but motorised vehicles gave them the opportunity to do things on a bigger and wider scale. Three wheels, four or more, the GWR used all combinations for all sorts of services in its 'motorised' section. Here is shown a three-wheeled express parcels cart. (David Hyde Collection)

➤➤ A 20hp Milnes Daimler GWR bus waiting for exiting train passengers at Marlborough Station, c.1904. (David Hyde Collection)

▶ The First World War was an opportunity for women to do jobs they had never done before, including the excitement of driving motor vehicles. During the Second World War GWR women not only drove a variety of motorised vehicles, they maintained and repaired them too. (David Hyde Collection)

Most today are familiar with the 'Seven Wonders of the World', but many would argue over the line-up of the 'Seven Wonders of the GWR'! There are certain 'iconic' elements that trip off the tongue without pause for thought. That they do so is because they are 'wonders' of the railway and engineering worlds. Here, in no particular order, are seven that would probably 'trip off the tongue'...

1) THE ROYAL ALBERT BRIDGE

The Royal Albert Bridge across the River Tamar at Saltash, between Plymouth and Truro, was Brunel's last engineering masterpiece. Built to join the Cornwall Railway to the rest of the broad gauge system this 'bowstring suspension bridge' celebrated its 150th year in 2009.

The technical criteria to be met were demanding. The bridge needed to be supported 80ft below mean sea level, have a minimum headway of 100ft to allow tall ships to pass under, breach the 1,100ft-wide river, and carry heavy, thundering train loads.

The two main spans are based on the principle of a suspension bridge, making the structure unique, as to this day, it is the only one of its type that carries mainline trains. In simplistic terms Brunel designed a double-span bridge (each span being 455ft) with long approach viaducts, but what he produced with its 'tied-arch' construction is one of the most superiorly engineered, breathtaking structures in the history of bridge design. Opened with pomp and ceremony by Prince Albert on 2 May 1859, the bridge is still attracting admiring visitors.

(David Hyde Collection)

 (Great Western Trust Collection)

The ROYAL ALBERT BRIDGE, SALTASH
Brunel's famous link between Glorious Devon and The Cornish Riviera

78

Saltash. Royal Albert Bridge.

2) BOX TUNNEL

Box Hill was a formidable barrier to the GWR mainline between Bath and Swindon, not least because of its geological make-up of a type of limestone better known as Bath Stone. Undoubtedly seen as a Brunel masterpiece today, there were many detractors at the time who foresaw only calamity, with fears that passengers would be suffocated travelling through its long length!

It was a project that encountered monumental difficulties, expensive in cost and in lives. Of the 4,000 who men who worked there over the five-year construction period, it is said that some 100 lost their lives whilst many others were maimed.

Work started in 1836 with the sinking of eleven shafts. Then excavation was started from each end. It was a matter of gunpowder blasts and picks and shovels. The initial flooding problems were overcome by using steam pumps. Work was continuous, with one shift relieving the other. Over 30 million bricks were used, although not all the tunnel was lined with them.

Completed in 1841, the tunnel measures 1 mile 1,452yds (2,937m) long, is straight, and descends a 1 in 100 gradient from the east. The western portal (Box end) is in a dramatic classical style, whilst the Corsham end was built with a simple, plain brick face. Whilst not the longest tunnel in the world, it was the longest railway tunnel in the world at that time. On certain days of the year, usually in April, part of the rising sun can be seen shining right through the tunnel!

3) THE SEVERN TUNNEL

The Severn Tunnel links the west of England to South Wales by going under the River Severn at a place known as 'the Shoots', a narrow but unusually deep section of the river.

➤ *An express train for South Wales leaving the tunnel.*

It is a wonderful example of 'if at first you don't succeed try, try, and try again'. It took almost thirteen unlucky years between March 1873 and January 1886 to complete and for the first train to run. Only 2¼ miles of the tunnel is actually under water, yet the most persistent problem that held up construction was the invasion of water, particularly from the Welsh side at a point that came to be known as 'the Great Spring'.

Eventually the 4-mile, 624yd (7,008m) tunnel was completed in 1885 and the first goods train passed through in January 1886, followed by passenger traffic in December 1886. For over 100 years it remained the longest mainline railway tunnel in the UK.

4) PADDINGTON STATION

One of the most charismatic of all the Victorian railway stations, Paddington has managed to keep its character and spirit whilst evolving to meet modern-day demands. Brunel was on the Building Committee of the Crystal Palace for the Great Exhibition of 1851, and this experience greatly influenced his vision for his iconic terminus.

Brunel wrote to Sir Matthew Digby, the architect who had overseen the construction of Crystal Palace, inviting his collaboration:

I am going to design… a Station after my own fancy… with engineering roofs, etc… such a thing will be entirely *metal* as to all the general forms… it almost of necessity becomes an Engineering Work… but for *detail* of ornamentation I neither have time nor knowledge…'

DOMINE DIRIGE NOS

VIRTUTE ET INDUSTRIA

PADDINGTON STATION

Therefore much of the architectural detailing was done by Digby. The contractors Fox, Henderson & Company, who had built Crystal Palace, were also engaged.

This spectacular train shed, built from 1851–54 to facilitate GWR's broad gauge trains, has a soaring roof with three barrel vaults of clear arch construction. These have 189 decorative wrought iron ribs and were supported by a cast-iron column for every third rib. The roof is 699ft (213m) long. The original roof spans had two transepts connecting the three spans.

In the typical GWR fashion of doing things 'their way', Paddington Station is unusual in that it did not have a principal exterior façade; instead there was the Great Western Hotel. Opened on 16 January

1854, the total build cost (including the Goods Depot and Carriage Department) is said to have been around £600,000.

A fourth bay was added in 1916 in keeping with the style but with steel hexagonal columns. Between 1916 and 1924 all the cast-iron columns were replaced with these new steel columns. Brunel is immortalised in his still magnificent station with a seated statue that can be seen beside the side entrance to Platform One.

▲ *(David Hyde Collection)*

◄◄ *(David Hyde Collection)*

5) THE ROUTE

The railroad that Brunel created from Bristol to London, bookended by the magnificent showcases of grandeur, the termini of Bristol Temple Meads and Paddington Station, has often been described as a masterpeice. It incorporates so many individually incredible pieces of engineering. Brunel himself described it as 'the finest work in the kingdom'.

The route of 118 miles and 38 chains (via Box) (just 44 yards off 188½ miles), is sometimes called Brunel's 'billiard table'. It was a Pandora's box of challenges. The line sets out from Paddington in confident mood and is soon carried high over the River Brent on the eight semi-eliptical arches of Warncliffe Viaduct, built in 1837. It crosses the River Thames three times, the first of these at the 'beggar's belief' Maidenhead Bridge, then again by the Gatehampton and Moulsford Bridges. The impressive Sonning Cutting, which was pushed straight as a die through Sonning Hill, is a victory of man and muscle over daunting Mother Earth. No machine was used in the making of it, just spades, wheelbarrows and horse-drawn carts! It took a muscle-aching two years to complete.

The most difficult section of the line to construct was the section from Bristol to just west of Box. This 18 miles involved the cutting of no fewer than seven tunnels – Box Tunnel being the longest and most difficult – three viaducts and four major bridges. The run of the line to the east of Bathwick Hill through Sydney Gardens has been described as 'perhaps the most graceful railway townscape in the country'.[1] Yet it is not just the engineering feats and the smooth, fast ride through the landscape that sets this route apart and singles it out as 'remarkable'. It is also the cultural context of its railway buildings and architecture, all reflecting the influence of their situation. It thoroughly deserves its proposal as a Unesco World Heritage Site.

◀ *St James Bridge and Station, Bath.*

➤ *This atmospheric photograph shows the Maidenhead Bridge with centering wooden supports having been placed in position in readiness for the bridge's extension on the southern side. It brings to mind the story of Brunel duping his public critics, who maintained that such a low-rise bridge could not be self-supported. Brunel left up his wooden support structure but short of actually doing any supporting. It wasn't until some months later when this was swept away in a storm that people realised what the true situation had been!*

6) MAIDENHEAD BRIDGE

The 'wonder' of Brunel's Maidenhead Bridge was its simplicity and boldness. The bridge, with two elegant brick arches, spanned the River Thames near Maidenhead. Brunel was determined to keep his level gradient (1in in 1.320 at this stretch) and avoid a 'humped' bridge which traditional bridge building would have produced. It had a span of 128ft (39m), and a wondrously 'daring' rise from the springing of the arch to the crown, the highest point above water being a mere 24ft 3in (7m). At the time of its completion in 1839 it was the longest and flattest arched bridge in the world. Train services commenced over the bridge on 1 July 1839. Decades later the bridge was extended on the southern side to accommodate 4 tracks, after which it was officially opened to traffic on 4 June 1893.

7) 'KINGS' AND 'CASTLES'

When considering the 'wonders' of the GWR, talk must turn to its engines, especially those of the twentieth century and in particular the 'giants' – the 'Kings' and 'Castles'

➤ *So proud were the GWR of* King George V, *they shipped it to America as part of the Baltimore and Ohio Centenary Celebrations in 1927. The Americans were so enthusiastic about it that the Baltimore and Ohio Railroad Company presented it with a bell which was then always mounted gleaming on its front buffer beam.*

➤➤ King George V, *now a preserved 'heritage' piece at the National Rail Museum, York. (Bob Townsend Photographs)*

The aptly named 'Kings' class No.6000, (thirty were built in all) were the 'alpha males' of all the GWR engines. Designed by C.B. Collett, they were as exciting to the eye as they were in performance. These locomotives had Churchward's tapered boilers, copper-capped chimneys and brass bonnet safety valve covers, as well as four cylinders, two inside and two outside the frames. Supplied with steam at a pressure of 250lb per sq in, they were the GWR's most powerful express passenger locomotives, although they were described by some as 'weighty-puffers' that needed to be restricted from some lines! The first, and most famous, *King George V* outshopped at Swindon Works in 1927, is 68ft 2in long over the buffers, and in working order (with the tender) weighs 135 tons 14 cwt.

AND THREE THAT MADE THE TOP TEN

SWINDON WORKS

Many times in its life Swindon Works would proudly boast that it was 'probably the largest railway factory in the world!' This was no idle 'peacock-strutting'. At their largest capacity in 1929 the works covered an area of around 326 acres, including the mainlines running through them, and in 1924 employed over 14,000 people.

➤ This general view of Swindon Works during a normal working day c.1908 is full of interest. Note especially the ancient wagons and the newly repaired 1076 class 0-6-0 Saddletank by the turntable. Also shown is the new A Shop, opened in 1902, built on the site the BG 'Mortuary'. Apart from new construction and locomotive repairs, it housed a machine shop, wheel shop as well as the famed 'engine testing' plant. In 1921/2 this shop doubled in size when the A Shop extension was opened.

The company's original intention had been:

> To provide an Engine establishment at Swindon… where a change of engines may be advantageously made… [and which] would also comprehend the large repairing shops for the Locomotive Department…

But soon the company began to construct its own locomotives, carriages and wagons. The Works operated three sections. Locomotive came first. Carriage & Wagon came together later and were always spoken of in one breath. Swindon Works came to have a worldwide reputation.

▲ *This unusual and rare coloured depiction of the inside of Old Oak Common Shed shows off its full glory in pristine opening condition. Four engines stand posed to hammer home the information that this shed houses not just one, but* four *massive turntables.*

OLD OAK COMMON LOCOMOTIVE SHED

Not content in designing spectacular engines, Churchward also designed a spectacular shed for them. Old Oak Common was the largest depot on the system when finished in March 1906. It was the largest of its type in the country 'and probably the world' boasted the company magazine! It was the prototype 'internal turntable' depot, housing four impressive 65ft-diameter turntables under one roof and it set the standard for future practice.

THE BROAD GAUGE

For sheer audacity in a land of railway conformity, one cannot but admire the broad gauge. Its 'extreme width', as described by the Board, made it unique and immediately established the GWR's

➤ *This picture of Wootton Basset incline perfectly illustrates the enormous width of the broad gauge track. In the middle ground on the left can be seen a 'bobby' box. Before the introduction of signals, the 'bobby' had to ensure the safe running of the trains. Later, when signalmen took over the responsibility of signalling the trains through, these boxes became signal boxes and the 'bobbies' became the Transport Police.*

future reputation of being 'different' to other railway companies. Its concept, way ahead of its time, would be more at-home in today's railway world, as discovered by more modern British Railways analysts.

A 'FLAVOUR' OF THE GWR

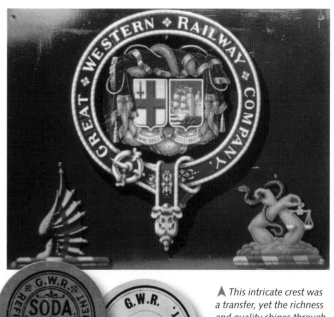

Great Western Railway.
HIKERS EXPRESS No.1
AVAILABLE FROM AND TO
PADDINGTON by SPECIAL TRAIN
FRIDAY MARCH 25th. 1932.
THIRD CLASS
4/0 Fare 4/0
Issued at Paddington 1
WD   See back

▲ The GWR ran many kinds of excursion 'Specials'. During the 1930s they had a big push on outdoor pursuits such as this one for 'Hikers' in 1932.

▶ GWR bottle tops produced at Swindon Works.

▲ This intricate crest was a transfer, yet the richness and quality shines through. It was used on the tenders, sides of coaches and early road vehicles up until c.1923. (All David Hyde Collection)

The GWR, known for its generally conservative nature, paradoxically was also radical and a real ground-breaker, as this list of 'firsts' shows.

'FIRSTS'

The GWR was the first railway to adopt 'standardisation' on a massive scale with Gooch's order of 105 six-wheeled tender engines of four classes between March 1840 and December 1842. He refused to accept the engine *Sun*, stating that 'she not being in conformity with our Drawings and Specifications... defeating our main object... to get our engines so that one part of any engine will fit another.'

TELEGRAPH LINES

It was a 'line' of a different sort that brought the GWR one of its earliest 'firsts'.

The GWR was the first railway company to install the new electric telegraph. The system was set up from Paddington Station to West Drayton as early as 1839 and it had reached Slough by 1843. In January 1845 it played a splendid role in apprehending a murderer who was making his escape by train from Slough. The telegraph was used to alert the police at Paddington that the murderer, John Tawell, had bought a first class ticket to that station. Tawell was arrested on arrival and eventually hanged.

Strangely, the GWR made only half-hearted use of the invention for general business and only used it for signalling trains through one or two long tunnels, such as Box. In 1850 the GWR Directors at last realised the benefits of electric communication and entered into contracts with the ETC, who had bought up Cooke

◄ *Simple beginnings for something that was to become amazingly big and significant. So great was the public interest in this invention that a fee of one shilling was charged for admission. The Electric Telegraph Station at Slough. (David Hyde Collection)*

and Wheatstone's patents. The telegraph was brought into use between Oxford and Banbury in October 1850 and the whole route from Paddington to Bristol was equipped in May 1852. In May 1855 the GWR established their own Telegraph Department with Mr C.E. Spagnoletti, an ex-ETC employee, as Head of Department, paying him a handsome £100 a year. In 1910 the GWR modestly wrote, 'it needed no great foresight to perceive that the telegraph and telephone would become such important factors in the conduct of railway work'.

'WATCH THE CLOCK!'

In the early days of the railways, time was still set locally, so it varied down the line. The GWR were the first to introduce a standard time to their system, which they called 'London Time' as it was initially set from Paddington. Local communities called it 'Railway' or 'Station Time' as it was taken from the big outside clock visible on all stations. These clocks were obligatory by law.

TRAINS

The GWR pulled the first Royal train. The *Illustrated London News'* report of Queen Victoria's first rail journey on 13 June 1842 stated, 'Queen Victoria abundantly attended by fashionably dressed ladies, took the special train from Slough to Paddington Station on the Great Western Railway line, the whole journey [18¼ miles] having taken a mere 25 minutes (time of arrival being 12:25 p.m.)'. Victoria was greatly taken with the journey (she was driven by Gooch who was accompanied on the footplate by Brunel) and with the specially built carriage

◄ *Queen Victoria was the first reigning monarch to travel by train. She declared herself 'quite charmed' by it all. This well-known depiction of her travelling is not assigned to any particular railway company.*

provided by the GWR. Victoria also made
her last railway journey on the GWR when
her remains were conveyed for burial.

The **'Special Postal' trains** put on from 1 February 1855 between Paddington and Bristol were the first in the world. The Travelling Post Office (TPO) trains only travelled at night, so were rarely seen. Decades later some of the coaches on these trains could pick up and drop off mail bags without the train even slowing down!

Britain's first 'corridor train' (with toilet facilities) went into service on the GWR on 1 October 1892. It ran from Paddington to Birkenhead and heralded a new age of comfort for passengers.

In 1904 the 'Cornish Riviera Express' started making the world's longest non-stop run, over 245 miles (224¾ after the Castle Cary & Westbury route opened in July 1906) between Paddington and Plymouth. The GWR kept this distinction for nearly a quarter of a century!

◄ *'Corridor trains' have become a well-loved institution. This shows the wonderful variety of woods that were used in their internal construction around 1920. (David Hyde Collection)*

◄◄ *The GWR liked to present itself as 'The Royal Line', as the royal family travelled with it so often. This is the pre-1897 Royal Train showing the Queen's new carriage (1897) fourth from the locomotive, whilst the fifth carriage is her previous one. (GWR/ David Hyde Collection)*

➤➤ *So impressive was the record-breaking 'Cheltenham Flyer', it had its own 'books for boys of all ages' publication.*

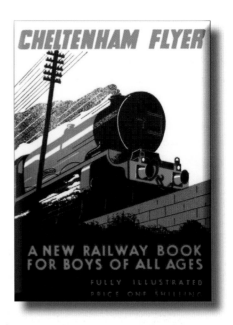

SPOTTER'S BOOK

Probably the most-loved train book ever printed by any railway company! The GWR produced the very first train spotters' guide, *G.W.R. Engines – Names, Numbers, Types and Classes* (commonly called 'the Engine Book'). It was an overwhelming success and ran to many editions.

'PACIFICS'

1908 was a spectacular year of locomotive milestones. In February that year the GWR unveiled a new engine, 'Pacific' No.111 *Great Bear*. She was the first, and for several years the only 4-6-2 tender engine

◀ *'Pacific' class 111* Great Bear *excited the imagination of the public and railway enthusiasts alike. People loved to see it, especially working out of Paddington as seen here* c.1914.

of its kind in Great Britain and the only one of that type the GWR ever produced. Built, it is said, to satisfy demands from the directors for the prestige of having the largest locomotive in Britain, she had four high-pressure cylinders fitted with piston-valves. Whilst the driving, or rigid wheel-base had been reduced to 14ft, a pair of inside bearing wheels were added, along with the tender and its new two four-wheeled bogies. She caused much debate. Undoubtedly she was the GWR's new 'glamour queen'. Fully lined out with brass splasher beading and copper cap to chimney, she was a wonderful piece of PR for the company and enthusiasts would flock to Paddington to catch a glimpse of her.

EXPRESS TRAINS

Commonly and affectionately known as the 'Cheltenham Flyer', the 'Cheltenham Spa Express' became the first normal daily passenger train in the world to be scheduled at over 70mph (110km/h) in 1923. It left Cheltenham at 2.30 p.m. every weekday (later on at 2.40 p.m.). Its schedule for the 77¼ miles (124.3km) was 75 minutes in 1923, but this was later reduced to 70 minutes and then just 65 minutes in May 1932.

◄ *Just 'one-of-a-kind' the* Great Bear, *seen here in its photographic 'grey' before being finished in its proper colours and trim, makes an imposing image. Whilst it intrigued the public as well as the railway world, it is said that Churchward himself was not fully happy with it and was not sad to see this 'Pacific' class 'let go'. (David Hyde Collection)*

◀ Top: the famous first headboard. Below: the half-round board which replaced it in 1936. (Bob Townsend Collection)

◀◀ The record-breaking 'Cheltenham Flyer' flys over the 4 track Maidenhead Bridge on the mainline to Paddington. The 'Record of Records' is said to have been set on 6 June 1932 with engine 5006 Tregenna Castle. Driver Ruddock and Fireman Thorp brought home a time of 56 minutes and 47 seconds with a top speed of 91.4mph! This was the picture used for the 'Cheltenham Flyer' jigsaw puzzle which proved to be the most popular GWR puzzle of all! (David Hyde Collection)

Early GWR bus AF84, c.1904, working service from Helston Railway Station to The Lizard, Cornwall.

➤ *(David Hyde Collection)*

BUSES

A most unusual 'first' for a railway company! The GWR started its own 'road-motors' (as it called them) bus service (or even 'railway motor services') between Helston Railway Station and The Lizard on 17 August 1903. These company coloured buses in 'chocolate and cream' operated throughout the GWR terrritory on railway feeder services and excursions. Around the 1930s they were transferred to local bus companies, mostly those in which the GWR held shares.

➤ *The GWR was determined not to be thwarted by the rise of the motor vehicle – they simply created a 'motorised road' section of the company. These stylised depictions of vehicles show the changes in company branding over the years. (Great Western Trust Collection)*

MORRIS COMMERCIAL SALOON OMNIBUS of 1928.

SCAMMELL 6-TON TRACTOR with DYAK 'G' TRAILER and CONTAINER of 1936.

(Great Western Trust Collection)

AIR TRAVEL

Yet another unusual 'first', air travel became part of the GWR portfolio on 12 April 1933 when it inaugurated the world's first railway sponsored air service between Cardiff and Torquay, and Plymouth. The first plane was a Westland Wessex monoplane, supplied by Imperial Airways and specially painted in the GWR colours. It had three engines but could carry only six passengers. Later de Havilland Dragon Rapide aircraft were used. The flight was a whole lot quicker than the four-hour or so equivalent journey by train running to Bristol, then south-west to Devon. Initially there were two flights a week in each direction. This short flight route soon expanded into others across the GWR system. This service was operated by Railway Air Services from 7 May 1934.

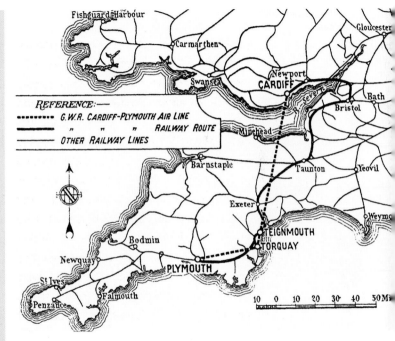

GREAT WESTERN RAILWAY
AIR SERVICES

Commencing April 12th, 1933, the Great Western Railway Company will inaugurate an Air Service between

PLYMOUTH (Plymouth Air Port)
TORQUAY & TEIGNMOUTH
(Haldon Aerodrome)
and **CARDIFF** (Air Port)

FLYING TIME

From Plymouth Air Port	From Haldon Aerodrome
75 Minutes	**50** Minutes

**Imperial Airways Westland Wessex
6-Seater 3-Engined Air Liner & Pilot·**

HEAVY LUGGAGE COLLECTED. CONVEYED BY
RAIL AND DELIVERED WITHOUT EXTRA CHARGE

**Special bus services connecting
Stations and Aerodromes**

FARES to CARDIFF	FROM	Single	Return
	PLYMOUTH AIR PORT AND BUS FROM PLYMOUTH, MILLBAY STATION	£3-10/	£6
PHONE CARDIFF 8100	HALDON AERODROME AND BUS FROM TEIGNMOUTH AND TORQUAY	£3	£5

Paddington, London, W 2.   JAMES MILNE, General Manager

REFERENCE:—
•••••••• G.W.R. CARDIFF-PLYMOUTH AIR LINE
———— " " " RAILWAY ROUTE
———— OTHER RAILWAY LINES

◄▲ *(David Hyde Collection)*

111

SALESWOMAN

Bold and radical again, in 1936 the GWR employed the first 'saleswoman' to act for a British railway company. Miss Audrey Shirliff's duties were to 'keep in touch with all kinds of women's organisations, works and factories where women are employed in order to assist in the promotion of outings and excursions', offering advice on 'itineraries, sight-seeing, amusements and catering'.

'RECORD BREAKERS'

TUNNEL

The Severn Tunnel between Bristol and South Wales is 4 miles 624yds (7,008m) long, although only 2¼ miles (3.62km) of the tunnel is actually under the river. Opened in 1886, it was the longest under-water railway tunnel within the UK for over 100 years.

NON-STOP RUN

The world's longest non-stop run from Paddington to Plymouth, named the 'Cornish Riviera Express', was introduced on 1 July 1904.

➤ 'Star' class locomotive pulling the 'Cornish Riviera Limited Express' at full speed. The 'dreadnought' coaches, built in 1904, were named after the battleship of the time and were in use up to the 1950s; the brown livery was only in use between 1908–12.

100MPH SPEED RECORD

Built in 1903, *City of Truro* No.3717, one of Churchward's powerful 'City' 3700 class built for hauling express trains, gained immortality by reportedly becoming the first locomotive in the world to reach the speed of 100mph (160kph) on 9 May 1904. It is said to have reached a speed

◀ *The record-breaking No.3440 City of Truro, now a 'heritage' piece and part of the National Collection.*

of 102.3mph (164kph) whilst hauling the 'Ocean Mails Express' down Wellington Bank. Because of this historical record it was preserved at York Museum in 1931 and is now part of the National Collection at the National Rail Museum.

DOCKS

Under the Railways Act 1921 the newly amalgamated GWR had become the largest dock-owning company in the world.

100 YEARS

Having survived the re-grouping and kept its name and identity in 1921, in 1935 the GWR became the only one of the mainline railways in this country to achieve its centenary. It eventually had a lifespan of 112 years.

Whilst the GWR started life purely as a railway company it grew to own many different transport 'parts': rail – road – air – and sea!

In 1871 it was granted Parliamentary permission to operate ships. It eventually established a significant shipping service. It ran shipping services from Weymouth to the Channel Islands and Fishguard to Rosslare, Ireland. Many of its ships saw active service during the two world wars, one, the SS *St Patrick* was bombed and sunk by German aircraft on 13 June 1941 with the loss of thirty lives, passengers and crew. It was a black day for the people of Fishguard. For her bravery in saving women passengers trapped on the lower deck, stewardess Miss Elizabeth May Owen was awarded the George Medal. The ship's recovered battle-scarred pennant is shown here.

▼ *The* Roebuck *(1) was built in 1897 for the GWR's Weymouth–Channel Islands services. In 1914 she was commandeered for active service and became HMS* Roedean. *She sank in 1915 after a collision.*

▲ The GWR also ran a steamboat ferry across the River Dart between Kingswear and Dartmouth known as The Mew (seen working here in 1939) as a connecting services for trains departing from Kingswear. She carried passengers, vehicles and livestock.

GREAT WESTERN RAILWAY
The Direct Route to IRELAND VIA FISHGUARD
TO BE OPENED IN SUMMER 1906

ST PATRICK

1833

(21 January) Business men of Bristol meet to discuss possibility of a Bristol to London
Railroad

(7 March) Isambard Kingdom Brunel appointed as engineer to survey the route.

(19 August) First joint meeting of Bristol and London Committees.

Title 'Great Western Railway' adopted.

1834

(25 July) GWR Bill rejected on grounds of 'insufficient means'.

New prospectus issued to raise more funds.

1835

(31 August) Great Western Railway Act passed by Parliament. This does not stipulate the
gauge width!

(29 October) Birth of the broad gauge. Directors resolved that 'the embankments, bridges
and other works to be constructed of such dimensions as to admit rails being laid to the
extreme width proposed by Mr Brunel, viz., 7ft' (¼ inch added for expansion).

1836

Work commenced.

1837
(18 August) Daniel Gooch appointed Locomotive Superintendent.

1838
First GWR train ran as a 'Director's Special', hauled by the engine *North Star*.

1839
(1 July) Maidenhead–Twyford section opened.

1840
Much of the line completed, only Swindon–Bath section remaining.
(16 December) line reached Swindon.

1841
(30 June) London-Bristol line fully opened. First train ran from Paddington to Bristol in 4 hours. Network had 170 miles of broad gauge track.

1843
(2 January) Swindon Works opened for business.
Brunel's great iron ship SS *Great Britain* launched in Bristol.

1845

'Break of Gauge' controversy instigates Gauge Commission.

1846

(February) First complete engine to be built by the company – Great Western – completed.
Gauge Commission finds in favour of the 'narrow' gauge 4ft 8 ½ins. This becomes the
  'standard' gauge for all new railways.

1847

GWR Medical Fund Society started in Swindon.

1848

(14 June) Swindon Works 'Trip' commenced.

1854

GWR absorb the Shrewsbury & Chester Railway, acquiring standard gauge locomotives
  and rolling stock.

1855

First 'narrow' gauge locomotive built at Swindon.
First 'Special Postal' train run by GWR.

1859

(2 May) Royal Albert Bridge at Saltash, designed by Brunel, is opened.

1866

(November) Daniel Gooch becomes Chairman of the Board.

1871

Powers granted by Parliament for GWR to operate ships.

1874

Work begins on the Severn Tunnel

1875

The vacuum brake employed on passenger rolling stock. This was a safety system that applied a train's brakes if it passed a danger signal.

1877

Last broad gauge branch line opened to St Ives.

1886

The Severn Tunnel opens – Britain's longest underwater mainline tunnel.

1892

First corridor train with toilet facilities runs.

(21–22 May) Last of the broad gauge changed to standard gauge.

1895

Compulsory ten-minute stop at Swindon Station ended when GWR bought back the catering concession.

1903

(10 March) First non-stop run between Paddington and Plymouth via Bristol with the Royal Special.

(17 August) Start of GWR's own road motor services.

1904

City of Truro becomes first locomotive in the world to reach 100mph.

1906

First use of 'Automatic Train Control' (ATC) during trials on the Henley branch line. Further trials carried out in 1908 (Paddington–Reading) and in 1909, after satisfactory trials on Lambourn section the GWR gave the go-ahead to introduce it throughout the system.
(17 March) Old Oak Common locomotive shed opened.

1914

(4 August) War declared. Government takes control of the railways.

1923

(1 January) All the railways are grouped into the 'Big Four'. The GWR was the only company to keep its own name and structure.

1933

(12 April) Introduction of air services from Cardiff to Torquay and Plymouth.
(4 December) GWR pioneered the use of diesel traction in the UK and introduced it in their fast railcars.

1934

(July) Introduction of the new GWR roundel.

1935

(31 August) GWR Centenary.

Introduction of 'The Bristolian'.

1939

The Second World War begins – Government takes control of railways again.

1946

The first oil-fired GWR locomotive appears and trials begin on gas-turbine propulsion.

1948

(1 January) Nationalisation of British railways.

(5 March) Last Board meeting of the Great Western Railway Company.

Did you know?

NEW LIMBS!

The GWR had a special workshop in Swindon Works that made artificial wooden limbs for those who lost their own in the service of the company. The first was probably in 1878 when an unfortunate man named Harris was run over by a train and had to have his legs cut off. Fortunately for Harris, he was a member of the Medical Fund Society who ordered him 'a pair of legs with sockets' – an engineering masterpiece. All limbs were customised to suit the individual's needs and interests and by the 1930s some 4,000 limbs had been issued.

Did you know?

MEDICAL FUND SOCIETY

The Medical Fund Society, said to be a forerunner of the National Health Service, started in Swindon Works during the tough year 1847. Its proud boast was that it looked after its members 'from the cradle to the grave', providing all the medical care they needed. It employed doctors, dentists, surgeons and opticians, and there was a pharmacy and hospital care, even Turkish, slipper and swimming baths for hygiene and morale. It also provided a horse and hearse for burials!

FLAGS

The GWR had its own flag. It had a white background and a broad red band at the top and bottom. In the middle of the flag was the company's crest (the arms of the cities of London and Bristol) in colour. The crest is enclosed within a decorative blue circle lined in yellow, in which the words 'Great Western Railway' appear in white, outlined in black.

It also had its own 'House' flag, very similar to the other, which was flown on the main mast of company vessels in port between sunrise and sunset.

SOURCES

ARTICLES

Copsey, J., 'On the 20th May…' *Great Western Railway Journal* (Vol.1, 1992–1993)

The Great Western Railway Magazine (1914–1918, 1934–1947)

The Railway Gazette Supplement – GWR Centenary (August 1935)

BOOKS

McDermott, E.T., *History of the Great Western Railway* (GWR Company, 1927)

The Locomotives of the Great Western Railway: Part Two – Broad Gauge

The RC&TS 1953

Matheson, R. *Railway Voices: 'Inside' Swindon Works* (The History Press, 2008)

Peck, A., *The Great Western at Swindon Works* (Oxford Publishing Company, 1983)

WEBSITES

Brunel University London: Broad Gauge Trilogy

Monmouthshire Railway Society 1985

The Broad Gauge Story

The Great Western Archive

Gauge Commission Evidence – Google

OTHER

Nock, O.S., 'Milestones in the GWR History' (Paper given 18 March 1971)

Matheson, R., 'Women and the Great Western Railway with Special Reference to Swindon Works'. (PhD thesis, 2002)